Science BOOSTER Book 6

Contents

How do I use this book
   to boost my performance? 2
Check your boost 4

AT2 Living things
Using words well ★ 6
Producers and consumers ★★ 7
Keys ★ 8
Measuring plant growth ★★ 9
Investigating soil conditions ★★ 10
Plant food ★★ 11
Planning a fair test ★★ 12
Writing a good conclusion ★★ 13
Designed to survive ★ 14
Repeating investigations ★ 15
Writing a good description ★ 16
Micro-organisms ★ 17
Micro-organisms are alive ★★ 18
Stopping germs spread ★★ 19
Graphic conclusions ★★ 20
A table of results ★ 21

AT3 Materials
Explaining well ★ 22
Dissolving/evaporating ★ 23
Quick dissolving ★★ 24
Fair testing ★★ 25
Making bar charts ★★ 26
A safe investigation ★ 27
Reversible changes ★ 28
Making new materials ★★ 29
Anomalous results ★★ 30

AT4 Physical processes
Writing instructions ★ 31
Weight is a force ★ 32
Everyday forces ★★ 33
Forces ★★ 34
Using graphs ★★ 35
Shadows ★ 36
Paths of light ★★ 37
Shadows/reflections ★★ 38
Predicting ★★ 39
Improving explanations ★★ 40
Electrical words ★ 41
Electrical symbols ★ 42
Drawing circuits ★★ 43
Matching circuits ★★ 44
Controlling with switches ★★ 45
Confusing words ★ 46

Glossary 47

How do I use this book to boost my performance?

Each unit in this book is set out in the same way. Each one will help boost your understanding of science and become better at investigations.

The questions and activities in each unit can be done as part of normal class work or for homework in the form of a booster lesson.

Each of the units should fit in with the work you are doing in Year 6.

To help you get the best out of the book:

- read each unit slowly and carefully. Give yourself time to think about the ideas.
- work closely with your teacher or friends so that you share each other's ideas.
- do all of the activities in the order they have been set out. This will help you feel the boost.
- go back to any units you find difficult a few days later, after the ideas have had time to sink in.
- if you don't understand what something means, ask someone who can help you with it.

Key idea
Don't ignore this key idea. It tells you the most important idea in the unit.

Each unit has a star rating
☆ A one-star unit has been written to ensure you are working at Level 4 in Year 6.
☆☆ A two-star unit has been written to help boost your performance to a higher level.

Warm up
This task should take around five to ten minutes. It will help you and your teacher to get your brain working and to start to identify how much you need boosting.

Lift off
This activity will take you about ten to 20 minutes to complete. In a one-star unit it often revisits an idea you have come across before. In a two-star unit it helps you think about an idea you have recently learned.

The booster
This activity will also take around ten to 20 minutes to complete. It is harder than the 'Lift off' activity and, if you do it well, it will help to boost your understanding or skills to a higher level.

Paths of light ★★

Ray diagrams show how light travels

Warm up — Which of the following are sources of light?

- the Sun
- a flower
- aluminium foil
- the Moon
- fire
- a candle
- a mirror
- a television

Lift off — For the boy to see the cat, light rays from a source must bounce off the cat and go into his eyes.

Which of these diagrams shows how the boy sees the cat?

The booster — There is one big mistake in each of these ray diagrams.

Light rays are drawn as straight lines. There is one arrowhead in the middle, which shows the direction the light travels.

Explain why each diagram is wrong.

Checkpoint — Now let's see if you can draw ray diagrams of your own.

Draw diagrams to show how:

a light travels from the Sun to a tree and into your eyes
b you can see around a corner using a mirror
c you see yourself in a mirror
d you see the Moon
e a shadow is formed.

Checkpoint
Most of these activities take about five to ten minutes to complete, although some are a little longer. If you do this well, it means the boost has worked.

Top tips
These contain important information and tips to help you complete the activities.

Check your boost

What to do Make a copy of these two pages. Before you start your work, assess how well you think you can tackle each task.

Tick ☹ if you cannot do the task at all.

Tick 😐 if you can do some of the task.

Tick ☺ if you can already do the task well.

Focus on areas where you are weak first. As you complete each unit, try to convert a ☹ to a ☺. Mark it on your sheet. Keep a progress check on how many areas you have boosted.

Can you:	☹	😐	☺
state some words that mean one thing scientifically and another in everyday life?			
explain the difference between a consumer and a producer?			
use a key to name different plants and animals?			
use a graph to show how good your prediction was?			
set out information clearly in a table?			
describe what plants use to make their food?			
plan a fair test?			
write a good conclusion that includes an explanation?			
describe how some animals are suited to their habitats?			
explain why it is best to repeat investigations to get more results?			
write a good scientific description?			
name some micro-organisms that are helpful and some that are harmful?			
give some evidence to show that micro-organisms feed, grow and reproduce?			

Can you:	😞	😐	😊
explain how you would stop germs from spreading?			
draw conclusions from a graph?			
make a table of results?			
use the word 'because' to help explain a scientific idea?			
describe a situation where water evaporates from a solution leaving a deposit behind?			
explain how you would make a substance dissolve more quickly?			
set up a fair test?			
convert results from a table into a bar chart?			
plan a safe investigation?			
explain the difference between a reversible and an irreversible change?			
name some changes which make new materials?			
spot anomalous results on a graph?			
write clear and precise instructions on how to use a Newton meter?			
name and use the units of weight correctly?			
describe some examples where two forces act on an object at the same time?			
read some simple force diagrams correctly?			
write a scientific relationship using a graph?			
write clearly how to do an investigation?			
draw ray diagrams correctly?			
explain the differences between a shadow and a reflection?			
use a graph to predict new results?			
turn a bad explanation into a good one?			
use words to describe electrical circuits correctly?			
draw the correct symbols for a variety of electrical components?			
draw electrical circuits correctly?			
explain how to make bulbs brighter or dimmer using different numbers of cells in a circuit?			
draw some circuits that include a switch, and explain how they work?			
use scientific words without being confused by their spelling or meaning?			
use a glossary to help you understand the scientific words you use?			

Using words well ☆

Science words have a precise meaning

Warm up

Discuss the meaning of these scientific words or phrases.

adaptation   **habitat**   **food chain**   **interdependence**

Lift off

1 Match each word in the first column with its correct meaning in the second column.

predator   An animal that only eats meat.

consumers   Living things that use energy from the Sun to make their own food.

prey   An animal that only eats plants.

producers   Living things that eat other animals or plants.

herbivore   An animal that hunts and feeds on other animals.

carnivore   An animal that is eaten by other animals.

2 Write a better definition for each word.

The booster

Each of these words means one thing in science and something else in everyday life.

fertilise   **consumer**   **producer**   **key**   **suited**

Write two sentences for each word to show the two different meanings. Use a dictionary if this will help.

Checkpoint

Now see how well you can link the science words together.

Design and make a crossword about living things and how they depend on each other. Use as many science words from this page as you can. Use any others you know. For example:

1. An animal that is eaten by other animals.
2. An animal with a red, bushy tail.
3. An animal that eats other animals.
4. A wolf-like animal that 'laughs'.

	1.						2.
3.	p						f
	p	r	e	d	a	t	o	r
		e					x
4.	h	y	e	n	a		

6

Producers and consumers

Plants produce food. Animals consume it

Warm up
Copy and complete this passage using the words in the box.

| plants | zebra | prey | producers | consumers | predator | lion |

Some animals eat _____ and some eat other animals. All animals have to eat something, so they are called _____. An animal that catches other animals to eat is called a _____. The animals it catches are its _____. A _____ is a predator and a _____ is its prey. Plants such as grasses make their own food and so are called _____.

Lift off
Look at the animals and plants in this diagram. There are many food chains.

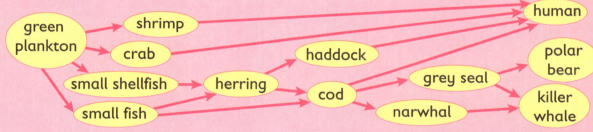

Here is one food chain: **green plankton → small fish → cod → human**

Find some more food chains in the diagram.

The booster
Now let's look at the details. There is only one producer in the diagram but many different consumers. The consumers might be predators or prey. Some can be both!

Producer	Consumer	
	Prey	Predator
Green plankton	Small fish	Cod

Sort out the animals and plants and put them in the correct column in the table.

Prey and predators all count as consumers because they all eat something.

Checkpoint
Think of a habitat near to where you live. A garden or park will do.

What are the producers and consumers in the habitat you have chosen?

7

Keys ★

You can find out the names of animals and plants using a key

Warm up A dog and an elephant have some things in common. For example, they both have four legs and they make milk for their babies.

List all the features by which you can tell them apart. For example, a dog is much smaller than an elephant. How many other differences can you think of?

Lift off This key leads to the names of the four birds shown in the box.

> duck   chicken   blackbird   sparrow

Follow and complete the key to find the names of the four birds.

Is it a large bird that often lives on a farm?

Yes ——————————————————— No

Does it swim on a pond?

Yes ——————— No

_____   _____

Is it black with a yellow beak?

Yes ——————— No

_____   _____

The booster Now make a key of your own.

Draw a key to lead to the names of the following fruits. Use the information given for each fruit to write your own questions for the key.

Apple	Grows on a tree	Green fruit
Orange	Grows on a tree	Orange fruit
Blackberry	Grows on a bush	Black fruit
Raspberry	Grows on a bush	Red fruit

When you make a key, try to use questions that split the group up with simple 'yes' or 'no' answers.

Checkpoint See if you can make a key from scratch.

Draw some keys of your own to name different things, for example:

coins   laboratory equipment   children in your class
butterflies   wild flowers

Measuring plant growth

Graphs show the pattern in observations

Warm up

All plants grow and then die.

1 Discuss the changes that take place in this plant as it grows. At which stages does it live off the food stored in the seed?

2 Where does its food come from in the other stages?

Lift off

Tom predicted that the roots of plants grow fastest when the first leaves of a plant open up and start to make food. Here are his results.

Length of root in mm					
	Plant 1	Plant 2	Plant 3	Plant 4	Plant 5
Day 0	0	0	0	0	0
Day 4	7	5.5	5	6.5	6
Day 8	8	10	11	17	12
Day 12	18	21	22	26	19
Day 16	22	24	28	32	34
Day 20	28	30	32	36	38
Day 24	30	32	34	36	32

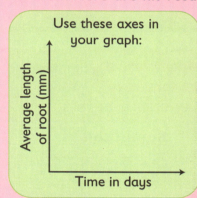

Use these axes in your graph:
Average length of root (mm)
Time in days

1 Work out the average length to which the roots grew in each four-day period.

2 Draw a graph showing how the roots grew over the 24 days.

The booster

Use your graph of Tom's results to say whether his results back up his prediction.

1 a Were there enough results?   b Why is it best to work out an average?

2 When were the roots growing the fastest?

3 Does this evidence fit your prediction? Explain why or why not.

Checkpoint

Now think about why graphs are important.

What advantage is there to looking at a graph rather than at figures in a table?

Investigating soil conditions Tables set out information clearly

Warm up Gather some samples of sandy, clay and loam soils.
1. Look at them using a hand lens or microscope.
2. Talk about what you see. Record any differences between the soils.

Lift off Different plants like different soil conditions.

Well-drained soil in the sun
in seed tray plant later

1. Study the information on seed packets, in gardening books or on garden and house plant labels.
   What types of soil does each plant prefer?
2. Use the information to draw up a table to show the kinds of plants that grow in sandy, loam or clay soils.

The booster Finding information in a table is easy if you study the information carefully. This table shows the properties of different kinds of soils.

Sandy soil	Clay soil	Loam soil
Larger particles	Fine particles	Mixture of particle sizes
Good drainage	Poor drainage	Reasonable drainage
Large air spaces	Few air spaces	Reasonable air spaces
Easily blown away	Acid	Rich in humus (dead plants)
Low in nutrients	High in nutrients	High in nutrients

Use the table to explain the main differences between the three types of soil.

Checkpoint Now the information is set out clearly, let's see if you can use it. Use the information to explain which of these soils would:
a provide a good home for worms
b enable plants to anchor themselves most effectively.

Plant food ★★

> Plants need air, water and light to make food

Warm up

Think about the questions below. Write one sentence to answer each one.

a Where did all the food you will eat today come from in the first place?
b Which foods come from animals and which come from plants?
c An egg comes from a chicken, but what does the chicken eat? Where does the chicken's food come from?

Lift off

Here is a simple food chain. The rose bush is called the 'producer' because it makes the food in the first place. Even the thrush relies on the food made by the rose.

rose bush → greenfly → ladybird → thrush

Which is the producer in these situations?

a A fox living mainly on rabbits that it catches.
b A baby calf drinking milk from a cow.
c A person eating mushrooms which grow in dead leaves.
d A kingfisher eating a fish it caught from a river.

Only green leaves can make their own food. They don't need to eat anything. They just collect simple things from the air and the soil and then turn them into food.

The booster

Now you know that plants are always the producers, you can go on to think about why. Plants make (produce) their own food out of a few simple things.

1 What simple things do plants need to make their own food?
2 If a plant is kept in the dark, it will die. Why is that?
3 Why does a plant need healthy roots to live?
4 Plants help animals by producing food for them. How do animals help plants?

Checkpoint

Now let's see if you understand how plants make their food.

1 Explain why green plants do not need to eat food to stay alive.
2 Which of these things does a green plant need to make its food?

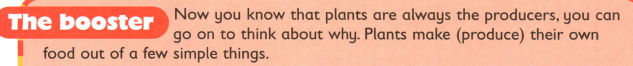

water   soil   air   warmth   compost   worms   sunlight   gravity

Planning a fair test ⭐⭐

Every test you plan must be fair

Warm up — Every scientific test must be fair. Which of these is the best meaning of a scientific fair test?

- Not copying anybody's results.
- Keeping everything the same in all your tests, apart from the one thing you are testing.
- Making sure all of the results come out the same each time.

Lift off — Mary wants to see if the amount of fertiliser she puts on her seeds makes any difference to how well they grow. She has three beakers of liquid with which to water her seeds. The three beakers contain different amounts of fertiliser.

List these stages of her plan in the best order:
- **A** Keep each dish watered with a different-strength fertiliser.
- **B** Label three dishes 1 to 3.
- **C** Measure how tall the seedlings in each dish have grown after one week.
- **D** Put some cress seeds in each dish.
- **E** Put paper in the dishes ready to grow the seeds on.

The booster — Now Mary has to make sure her test is fair. She needs to spot what she will keep the same and what she will change. She also has to decide what to measure.

Put these factors that Mary looked at in the correct column in the table.

- How much water she gives each seedling
- How near the window the three dishes are
- How often Mary waters the seedlings
- How tall the seedlings are
- The amount of fertiliser in the liquid
- How warm the dishes are

What she keeps the same	What she changes	What she measures

Checkpoint — You should now be able to answer this question.

If Mary had her three seed dishes standing in different parts of the room, it might confuse her investigation. Why is that?

12

Writing a good conclusion

Explaining a conclusion

Warm up
Sally's dad said that flowers never grew properly underneath his apple tree. Why do you think this might be?

Write two reasons why flowers might find it hard to grow under the apple tree.

Lift off
Sally thought that green plants needed light to grow properly. To test this, she put a brick on the lawn and left it for two days. The grass underneath the brick went very yellow and looked half dead.

Sally wrote this conclusion: *If a plant does not get enough light, it will die.*

Clare disagreed. She thought the lack of air was killing the grass. Clare drew this conclusion: *If a plant does not get enough air, it will die.*

They could both be right! The investigation wasn't good enough.

Describe how you could change the investigation to test *only* Sally's idea that plants need light, without getting it muddled up with whether air is also needed.

The booster
After trying an improved version of the investigation, Sally and Clare decided that plants do need light to survive.

Which of these would be the best scientific explanation for that fact?

- Sunlight makes a plant healthy.
- Darkness kills plants.
- Plants need sunlight to make their food.
- In the dark, plants think it is night-time and they go to sleep.

One of the answers is just silly and three of them are true in a way. Only one *really* tells us what is going on.

Checkpoint
Now see if you can write a conclusion which includes an explanation.

Sally and Clare grew some bean seeds in the dark. They thought they would die but were surprised when they grew quite well for a few days!

Complete the explanation: 'Seeds can grow quite well for a little while with no light because …'

Designed to survive ☆

Every habitat has animals suited to live there

Warm up

Humans do not live everywhere. For example, there is too little air high up a mountain and the North Pole is too cold; humans can't breathe under water and there is no food in the desert.

1 Name some animals that can live in places where humans would die.

2 How are these animals designed to help them live in these places?

Lift off

The place where animals and plants live is called their 'habitat'. There are many different habitats. The African jungle is one habitat and a desert is another. Each habitat has its own special animals and plants.

Draw a table like this one and fill it in. Think of **six** different habitats and name **two** animals that live in each one. The table has been started for you.

Habitat	Animal 1	Animal 2
African jungle	Chimpanzee	
Sahara Desert		

The booster

Now you need to think about why the animals are different in different places. Every animal has adapted so that it is suitable for its own habitat. For example, a polar bear has got very thick fur to keep it warm in the snowy Arctic, but it would be much too hot in Africa.

Animal	Habitat	How it has adapted
Polar bear	Snowy Arctic	Thick fur to keep it warm
Camel	Sahara Desert	
Flamingo	Lakes	
Squirrel	Woodland	
Mole	Underground	

Copy and complete the table to suggest one way that each of these animals is suited to its own habitat. One has been done for you.

Checkpoint

Consider in more detail where humans are best suited to live.

What would be the ideal habitat for a human being?

Repeating investigations

Investigations need to be made reliable

Warm up Write down all the ways you can think of that animals which live in cold places are especially suited to keep as warm as possible.

Lift off Is it really true that a furry coat keeps an animal warm?

Aidan decides to test this idea using beakers of warm water.

His idea is to wrap up a beaker in some furry material.

Will the water cool down more slowly in the wrapped beaker than in an unwrapped beaker?

1 What measurements should Aidan take? Think about:
   a how many measurements he should take altogether
   b how often he should take a reading.

2 Draw up a table of results that he could use to record his findings.

The booster Celia repeated Aidan's investigation but her unwrapped beaker cooled down much faster than Aidan's.

1 What could have happened to make Celia's results so different?

2 How could they make sure the problem did not happen again?

Checkpoint Let's see if you know the correct way to make investigations reliable.

Copy out these statements. Write 'reliable' next to the ones that will help to make your investigation accurate, and 'unreliable' if it will spoil your results.

a Let Celia and Aidan share the job of taking the temperature.
b Repeat the investigation under the same conditions.
c Always start at the same temperature.
d Do one test in the morning and the other at lunch time.
e Make sure you read the results accurately.
f Let the same person measure the temperature each time.

15

Writing a good description

A good description gives detail

Warm up

Write simple sentences to describe:

a what is in your schoolbag
b how you got to school today.

Lift off

How safe is this kitchen?

Talk to your friends for one minute and describe where you would find germs in a kitchen and what is happening to them. Choose your vocabulary carefully.

The booster

Redrafting often makes your descriptions better. Here is an example: 'Alan has fallen ill because some germs have attacked his body.'

Put the following ideas together in the correct order to tell the story of Alan falling ill and then getting better. Add your own details to improve the descriptions.

A He forgot to wash his knee and apply some ointment.
B Germs invaded his cut and attacked his body.
C As the germs were killed, new skin started to form under the scab on his knee.
D Once inside, the germs led to Alan having a temperature.
E After a day or so, Alan started to feel better.
F Alan's body defences (white blood cells) started to attack the germs.
G Alan grazed his knee playing football.
H After a while, the white blood cells killed all the germs.

Checkpoint

Now let's see if you can write a good description with plenty of detail. Remember, adding pictures with captions can also help you to describe things well.

Draw a cartoon strip showing how Alan grazed his knee and what happened to it afterwards. Make sure that you think carefully about the pictures and any captions.

Micro-organisms

Micro-organisms can cause illness and decay, but some are used to make food

Warm up

What are 'germs'? 'Germs' is an everyday word for 'micro-organisms'. There are many different kinds of micro-organism.

Find out and list some different kinds of micro-organisms.

Lift off

Some illnesses are caused by micro-organisms living inside us. You can catch these illnesses when germs move from someone else's body into your own.

Germs cause tooth decay. Get rid of those germs and your teeth will be healthy!

1. What ways do you know to remove germs from your mouth?
2. How can you stop them growing there in the first place?
3. Write down the names of some illnesses that are caused by micro-organisms.
4. Write down the names of some other illnesses that are *not* caused by germs.

The booster

Some micro-organisms do not cause illnesses and are useful. Even those that cause decay (rotting) have their good points. Others are used to make food!

1. Think about the germs that rot dead things.
    a. Describe one situation where decay is a problem for people.
    b. Describe one situation where it helps us when things decay.
2. A fungus called yeast is used to make bread. Fungus is a micro-organism. Find out some other foods made using micro-organisms.

Question 2 is a hard one. Think about farms and gardens.

Checkpoint

Now let's see if you know which germs are helpful and which are harmful.

Make a table to show which are which.

Helpful micro-organisms	Harmful micro-organisms
Yeast makes bread	Germs in the mouth cause tooth decay

17

Micro-organisms are alive

Micro-organisms feed, grow and reproduce

Warm up
Which of these do *all* living things do?

grow   fly   swim   reproduce   think   feed   move   speak

Lift off
Humans use a fungus, or micro-organism, called yeast to make bread and beer. The bubbles in beer are carbon dioxide gas made by the yeast.

1. In bread, what sign is there that yeast has been making carbon dioxide gas?
2. Why is it necessary to add sugar to the mixture when starting to make some bread or beer?
3. If the bread dough gets cold while it is being made, the bread will not rise. Why is that?
4. Cider is a 'fizzy' drink made from crushed apples. The yeast lives on the skin of the apple. Where does the sugar come from?

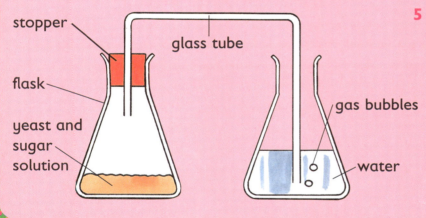

5. If you grow some yeast in this apparatus, you can see how much gas it makes by counting the bubbles.

   What would it do to the number of bubbles if you added more sugar to the yeast?

The booster
Now you have done the 'Lift off' activity, you can use your ideas to answer a more difficult question.

What evidence is there to show that yeast is alive?

Checkpoint
See if you understand some ways of controlling the growth of micro-organisms.

1. Explain why keeping food in a refrigerator helps to stop it going off.
2. Why is it important to do the washing up in hot water?

Stopping germs spread

Micro-organisms can spread

Warm up
Look at some packaged food from a supermarket, such as yoghurt. There is always a 'use by' date printed somewhere on the packet.

1. What does the term 'use by' mean?
2. What risks do you take if you ignore the label and eat something that is past its use by date?

Lift off
Think about what happens to an apple if it is left to stand for a few weeks.

1. What changes happen to the apple after a few days?
2. What is causing the apple to change in that way?
3. What would probably happen to you if you ate an apple that had 'gone off'? (Don't try it!)
4. What methods do people use to keep food fresh in their homes?

The booster
Now let's look at how you use this knowledge to stay healthy.

It is very important not to let micro-organisms get onto our food because they might cause food poisoning. That is why there are hygiene (cleanliness) rules in the kitchen. One example is: 'Always wash your hands before starting to cook.'

Write your own set of hygiene rules for the kitchen. Think about:

- Washing
- Cleaning
- Storage
- Using knives and chopping boards
- Pets

Remember, the whole point of these rules is to stop germs spreading from one sort of food to another.

Checkpoint
See if you know how to stop germs spreading.

After studying a list of hygiene rules, Sally realised that she should be stricter about washing her hands after using the toilet. Write down two changes you could make in your own life to stop germs spreading.

Graphic conclusions

Graphs give us a clearer picture of what our results really mean

Warm up

Yeast makes bubbles of gas as a waste product.

Which of these would be the best way to compare the amount of gas made by yeast samples that have been fed different amounts of sugar? Each one would work, but you have to say *why* you have made your choice.

- Counting the number of bubbles in a certain time.
- Weighing the flask to see how much gas had escaped.
- Catching the gas and measuring its volume.

Lift off

Darren was testing the idea: 'The more sugar I give to the yeast, the more gas it will make'. He planned to draw a graph of his results.

Darren had five identical yeast bubblers, each containing the same amount of yeast. The only difference was that each bubbler had a different amount of sugar.

Darren decided to use the 'bubble counting' method to test his idea. Here are his results:

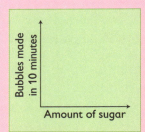

Amount of sugar	Number of bubbles made in ten minutes
1 spoon	20
2 spoons	35
3 spoons	42
4 spoons	45
5 spoons	45

Draw a graph using these axes and plot the points.

The booster

Now draw a smooth line through the points on the graph.

1. How many bubbles would there be in ten minutes if $2\frac{1}{2}$ spoons of sugar had been used?

2. What is the greatest amount of sugar it is worth giving to the yeast? Explain your answer.

Checkpoint

See if you can use Darren's graph to reach a better conclusion.

Look back to Darren's prediction. He was mostly right, but can you make a more accurate conclusion?

A table of results

Results have to be recorded clearly in a table

Warm up

Over a period of time, dead materials will rot away. These rotted materials can be used to make fertiliser for the soil. Gardeners make compost heaps to help micro-organisms rot their dead plants.

1. Discuss what makes a good compost heap.
2. How does a compost heap help the micro-organisms do their job?

Lift off

Penny measured the temperature inside of a pile of grass clippings. She knew that micro-organisms rot the grass and she wanted to see if they made any heat. Here are Penny's results:

> On Monday, the grass clippings were quite cold as they had been outside. They were only 17°C. On Tuesday, they were a bit warmer at 19°C. On Wednesday, the temperature was the same as Tuesday, but by Thursday it had reached 24°C. On Friday, it was 25°C. We were not at school on Saturday and Sunday, but on Monday it was up to 28°C. On Tuesday, it reached 30°C, but then dropped to 28°C for two days. It was cold then. On Friday, it went up to 34°C.

Penny's results look interesting and the clippings do seem to be getting warmer.

1. Why should Penny think about repeating her investigation?
2. Is there anything else she should have recorded as she went along?

The booster

With all of the words Penny has used, it is difficult to see what happened. She needs to set her data out much more clearly.

Draw a proper table of results to display Penny's data clearly.

Checkpoint

Now let's see if the data in your table is easy to use.

1. What were the lowest and highest temperatures recorded?
2. In the table, what is the best way to deal with the two 'missing' days – the Saturday and Sunday – in the middle of the investigation?
3. Do you agree with the statement that the compost heap is warming up?

Explaining well

'Because' is an important word to use when you are explaining

Warm up

Think about what the word 'explain' means.

1. Which of these statements tells you what is meant by the word 'explain'?
   - Write a description
   - Give a reason why something happened
   - Sort into groups
   - Say how one thing is similar to another

2. What is the difference between an explanation and a description?

Lift off

Some sugar is dissolving in water, but how do you know it is dissolving?

1. Think about what happens to sugar if you leave it in water.
2. Complete this sentence: 'You know the sugar is dissolving because …'
3. Compare your answer with that of your friends and try to improve your sentence.

The booster

There is more than one way to write an explanation – and practice makes perfect!

Add a sentence to each of these statements to explain each one better.

a. When water evaporates from a solution, solids are left behind.

b. The steam from evaporating seawater does not taste salty.

c. There is a limit to how much of a solid will dissolve in a particular volume of water.

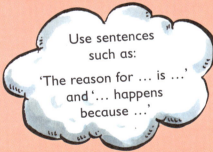

Use sentences such as:

'The reason for … is …' and '… happens because …'

Checkpoint

Now let's see how well you can explain something. Explainations need not be dull – you can use your imagination!

Pretend you are a small particle of solid salt being dissolved in water. Write an exciting account that explains why you dissolve more quickly in hot water than in cold. Don't forget to use the word 'because' in your sentences.

Dissolving/evaporating

 When water evaporates, anything dissolved in it is left behind

Warm up Does everything dissolve or can some things be put into water and just stay there without dissolving?

Discuss this with your group and make two lists:

Soluble substances (do dissolve)   **Insoluble substances (do not dissolve)**

Lift off Daniel's teacher boiled some salty water. She showed him how to collect pure water from the steam and how to get the salt back as well.

Put these sentences in the correct order.

A Collect the drops of water.
B Let the steam drift onto a cold mirror.
C Check the beaker for salt crystals.
D Boil some salty water.

The booster Daniel wanted to know if he could get the sugar in his tea back out again. He left some sweet tea overnight. In the morning, he saw some dry sugar left behind in the bottom of the cup.

Use the words in the box to complete Daniel's account of his investigation.

| dissolved | pure | solution | mixture | evaporate |

I knew that my tea had some sugar _____ in it. I wanted to know if I could get the sugar out of the _____ so I decided to let the water _____. I was left with sugar crystals in the bottom of the cup. The sugar was not as white as it looks in the packet, so I knew it was not completely _____. It was a _____ of sugar and other things that were in the tea.

Checkpoint Now let's see how well you understand these ideas.

1 What was left behind in each of Daniel's tests after the water evaporated?
2 Is the water made from the steam pure or does it have anything dissolved in it?

Quick dissolving

There are a few ways of affecting how quickly something dissolves

Warm up
Think about dissolving sugar in tea.

1. Do sugar lumps dissolve faster or slower than granulated sugar?
2. Does sugar dissolve faster in cold or hot tea?

Lift off
Mina wanted to know if sugar would dissolve faster in hot water. She had three beakers of water:

- Beaker 1 contained very cold water from the fridge.
- Beaker 2 contained normal tap water.
- Beaker 3 contained hot water.

Mina put one lump of sugar into each beaker.

1. Which sugar lump will dissolve the fastest?
2. Which sugar lump will dissolve the slowest?

The booster
This chart shows the results of a more complicated investigation into how quickly sugar dissolves. Look at the results carefully. Can you spot any patterns?

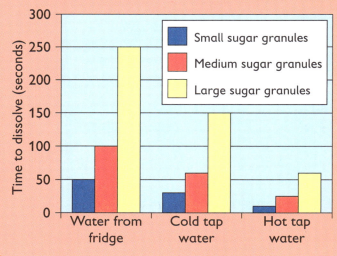

1. Which two different factors were being tested in the investigation?
2. Use the chart to complete these conclusions. Select the correct words in your answers.
    a. The hotter/colder the water, the faster/slower the sugar dissolves.
    b. The bigger/smaller the size of the sugar particles, the faster/slower it dissolves.

Checkpoint
Now let's see if you understand the ideas in this unit.

Mina noticed that her dad crumbled up a stock cube before trying to dissolve it. He was also using hot water. Explain why he did both these things.

Fair testing ⭐⭐

Any test you plan must be fair and clearly set out

Warm up

Can you write a plan to test the idea that 'small particles will dissolve faster than large ones'?

Which of these things belong in your plan?

- Improvements for next time
- Fair testing method
- The results
- A table for your results
- A prediction
- An outline of your method
- A conclusion
- A graph
- The equipment

Lift off

Think about what you will need and how you will do the test.

1   What equipment will you need? Choose from these:

stopwatch   beaker   spoon   stirring rod   Newton meter   kettle   magnet

2   List these main parts of the method in the correct order.

A Stop the stopwatch.

B Add exactly one level spoonful of sugar.

C Start the stopwatch.

D Put 50 cm³ of water in a beaker.

E Repeat the whole test with different sugars.

F Stir until all the sugar is dissolved.

The booster

Now think how you will make the test fair.

Look at these factors. One will be changed, some must be kept the same and one is the thing you are measuring. Put them in the right column in the table.

The temperature of the water
Whether you stir it or not
The time it takes to dissolve

The amount of water
The size of the sugar particles
The place you do the test

What you will keep the same	What you will change	What you will measure

Checkpoint

Now see if you can write all this up properly.

Use your answers to the questions to write your plan. Take especial care to explain how you will make your test a fair one.

25

Making bar charts ⭐⭐

Results from a table can be easier to understand in a bar chart

Warm up

Tom tried an investigation in which he timed how long it took for different types of salt to dissolve. He measured how long it took for one spoonful of each type to dissolve.

Which question was he testing?

- Rock salt is saltier than table salt.
- Sea salt is harder than rock salt.
- Small particles of salt will dissolve faster than large ones.
- The hotter the water, the faster the salt will dissolve.

Lift off

Here are Tom's results:

Salt type	Particle size	Time for one spoonful to dissolve
Ground-up salt	Very small	50 seconds
Table salt	Quite small	100 seconds
Sea salt	Medium	300 seconds
Rock salt	Large	700 seconds

1 Which kind of salt dissolved the fastest?

2 How long did it take the sea salt to dissolve?

3 How much faster does ground-up salt dissolve compared with table salt?

The booster

The results can also be set out in a bar chart. This makes it much easier to see what is happening.

Set out Tom's results for his dissolving investigation in a bar chart.

Put 'Particle size' along the bottom of your chart (the x-axis) and 'Time to dissolve' up the side (the y-axis).

Checkpoint

Now see how good a conclusion you can make from your bar chart.

Which of these would be a good conclusion to draw from the bar chart?
- Large particles dissolve more quickly than small ones.
- It makes no difference what size the particles are to how fast the salt dissolves.
- Small particles dissolve more quickly than large ones.

A safe investigation

You have to look after your own and everyone else's safety

Warm up — Spend five minutes brainstorming some of the things that might be dangerous in science practical work. For example, glass beakers might break and cut you.

Lift off — The children in Class 6 are investigating how well different substances dissolve. They were asked to measure how many spoonfuls of each substance will dissolve in 50 cm^3 of water.

Spot all the dangers in this picture. Make a list of them.

The booster — It is best to think about possible dangers before you start an investigation. You can then plan how to make it safe.

Make a table like this, to show how the dangerous things in the 'Lift off' picture could be put right.

What is dangerous?	How I would make it safe
The chemicals might react dangerously with water	Check with teacher first

Checkpoint — Now let's see if you know how to be safe in a practical lesson.

Write some science safety rules that could be pinned up in your classroom. One could be: 'Never eat sweets in a classroom where there are chemicals.'

27

Reversible changes ☆

Some changes are reversible; some are not

Warm up

When a car is in reverse gear, it goes backwards. We use 'reverse' in science when we talk about undoing something.

1 If we mixed up sand in some water, how could we reverse this?

2 Do you think it is possible to reverse a cake mixture?

Lift off

Look at all of these reversible changes. Match each one up with the way you could reverse it.

Change	How you could reverse it
Water freezing to ice	Using a magnet
Bath salts dissolving in water	Melting
Mixing large and small marbles together	Evaporation
Mixing up iron cans and aluminium cans	Sieving

The booster

If you melt chocolate it will set hard again if you let it cool. Boiling an egg is different. It doesn't turn it back into a raw egg if you let it cool down.

Sort out the changes in the box into 'reversible' and 'irreversible'. Enter them into a table like the one below.

> **dissolving salt in water**   **boiling an egg**   **burning a candle**
> **mixing iron filings and sand**   **melting chocolate**
> **charging a battery**   **dissolving chalk in vinegar**

Reversible	Irreversible
Melting chocolate	Boiling an egg

Checkpoint

Have you understood what the word 'reversible' means?

1 Write a sentence that says what the word 'reversible' means. Give one example of this.

2 Write a sentence that says what the word 'irreversible' means. Give one example of this.

Making new materials

Gases are sometimes made in irreversible changes

Warm up In reversible changes no new materials are made. For example, liquid chocolate is really the same stuff as solid chocolate.

Make a list of some more reversible changes in which no new materials are made.

Lift off Irreversible changes are different. In these changes, new materials are made and it is very hard to get back to the materials you started with. For example, when you burn wood, ash and smoke are made – ash and smoke cannot be turned back into wood.

What new materials are made in these irreversible changes?

Irreversible change	New materials made
Burning wood	Ash and smoke
Cement, sand and water	
Vinegar and bicarbonate of soda	
Burning a candle	

If you don't know the exact name of a new material, a description will do – 'bubbles of gas', for example.

The booster Sometimes the new materials that are made are gases.

Gases can be very dangerous. For example, when plastic burns, some of the gases are poisonous.

How could you tell if a gas is made when substances are mixed?

You are looking for a way of proving that a gas is there. You might say, 'Sometimes you can see bubbles.'

Checkpoint Do you know which reactions make gases? Which of these produces a gas when they are mixed?

- Plaster of Paris and water
- Lemon juice and washing powder
- Cement and water
- Vinegar and bicarbonate of soda

Anomalous results

Sometimes you need to be able to spot incorrect readings in results

Warm up Some numbers don't fit into a pattern. Spot the odd one out in each of these lists.

2   4   7   8   10

123   456   432   789

Lift off Sunita wanted to know how much gas was escaping as her candle burned. She decided to blow it out every ten minutes and measure its mass.

Here are her results:

Time in minutes	0	10	20	30	40	50
Mass of candle in grams	100	90	80	74	60	50

1. Plot a graph of her results using axes like the ones shown.

2. Which result does not seem to fit in with the others?

A result like this, that does not fit in with the rest, is called an 'anomalous' result.

The booster When you get a result which looks odd compared with the rest, you cannot just ignore it. You need to think about what might have caused it. Then repeat the investigation to see if it happens again.

1. What do you think might have caused the bad result that did not fit in with the rest?

2. With what should Sunita be careful when she repeats her investigation?

Checkpoint Now practise spotting some anomalous results.

Sunita repeated her investigation but there was still an anomalous result. Can you spot it? You might have to draw a graph to find it.

Time in minutes	0	10	20	30	40	50
Mass of candle in grams	98	83	81	70	61	49

Writing instructions

Instructions have to be clear, precise and correct if they are to work well

Warm up

1. Look at the ways in which instructions are written in cooking recipes, on food labels and on washing powder boxes.
2. List the points that make the instructions easy to use.

Lift off

If you want to use a Newton meter (force meter) accurately, you need to follow the correct instructions.

Write some instructions aimed at Year 5 pupils, to explain how to read the scales correctly on these two Newton meters.

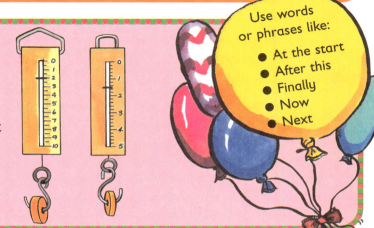

Use words or phrases like:
- At the start
- After this
- Finally
- Now
- Next

The booster

Redrafting can often make your instructions better. Now try this.

1. Compare your instructions with those of your friends. Discuss the strong and weak points of what you have each written.
2. Give each description a score out of 5 according to the following points.

   Score: 1 = brilliant, 3 = average, 5 = poor

Points to think about:

- Are the instructions clear?
- Are diagrams used to good effect?
- How easy is it to use the instructions?
- Are numbers used to order the instructions?
- Is each instruction well worded?
- Are the instructions in a good order?
- How well are phrases like 'At the start', 'Next', 'Then', 'After this' or 'When you have' used to give a sense of order?

Checkpoint

Let's see if you have learned how to write good instructions.

1. Make a display of the different instructions you and your friends have compiled.
2. Label each one with its good and not-so-good features.

31

Weight is a force

Weight is a force and is measured in Newtons

Warm up
Newton meters measure forces.
1. Use a Newton meter to weigh some everyday objects.
2. Devise a table to record your answers.

Lift off
Weight is a force. All objects have weight because the force of gravity pulls them towards the centre of the Earth. Study these diagrams carefully.

1. Which diagram correctly shows the direction in which gravity pulls?

Remember, gravity always pulls objects to the centre of the Earth. Do not just think it acts downwards.

2. Redraw the other diagrams to show the real direction in which gravity acts.

The booster
Forces are measured using a Newton meter (force meter). The precise unit for measuring weight is the Newton.

Name	Gary	Wayne	Ali	Dominic	John
Weight in Newtons	320	340	330	325	360

Name	Jessica	Rebecca	Mina	Sonia	Jade
Weight in Newtons	310	316	324	340	333

1. Make a bar chart of the children's weights.
2. What is the average weight of: **a** the boys? **b** the girls?
3. On average, do the boys weigh more than the girls?

Checkpoint
Now see if you understand the units of force.

An apple weighs 1 Newton. A child might weigh about 300 Newtons. Use these figures to estimate (guess) the weight of a shoe, a pencil case, this book and a coat. Measure the weight of each object to see if you guessed correctly.

Everyday forces ★★

> More than one force can act on an object

Warm up   There are many different kinds of force, such as gravity and friction.

How many other forces can you name?

Lift off   More than one force can act on an object. In picture 1, the ball is being pushed down by the hand and up by the upthrust of the water.

Write down the forces that act on the other objects in the pictures.

The booster   You can explain the motion of an object if you know the size and direction of the forces acting on it.

Gravity pulls the parachutist down, air resistance holds her back as she falls.

Write a caption for each stage of the parachutist's fall. Use the ideas of gravity, air resistance and speed.

Checkpoint   Now see how well you understand the two forces acting on the parachute.

Copy and complete this short paragraph using the words in the box.

| back   pulling   downwards   faster   air resistance   slower   gravity |

The force _____ the parachutist down is called _____. She would get _____ and _____ if that were the only force. Fortunately, _____ is another force acting on her which holds her _____. The force of gravity is larger than the _____ so she still falls _____ but at a much _____ speed.

33

Forces ★★

Force diagrams show the size and direction of forces acting on an object

Warm up

All forces have a size and a direction.

Copy and complete this paragraph using words from the box.

> Newtons   diagrams   scale
> bigger   describe   size
> arrowhead   longer   direction

To _____ a force well, you need to know how big it is and its direction. Force _____ are drawn to show both of these. The length of the arrow line, drawn to _____, represents the _____ of the force. The _____ the line, the _____ the force. The units of force are _____. The arrow is always drawn with an _____ at one end. The way in which the arrow points shows the _____ of the force.

Lift off

Lines are often drawn to scale to show the size of forces. You can work out the actual size of the force if you know the scale.

Use the scale 1 cm = 10 N to measure the size of these forces.

a →
b →
c →
d →
e →
f →

The booster

To describe a force fully, you need to say the direction it is pushing or pulling in.

Describe the direction the forces in the diagrams are acting in.

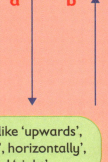
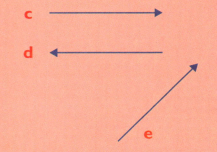

Use words like 'upwards', 'downwards', 'horizontally', 'left' and 'right'.

Checkpoint

Now see if you can read force diagrams correctly (still using the same scale).

Describe the size and direction of the two forces acting in this diagram.

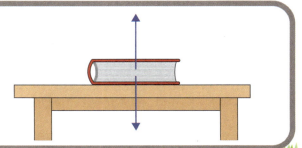

34

Using graphs ⭐⭐

The pattern shown by a graph can be used to write a relationship

Warm up

Adding weights to a spring causes it to get longer.

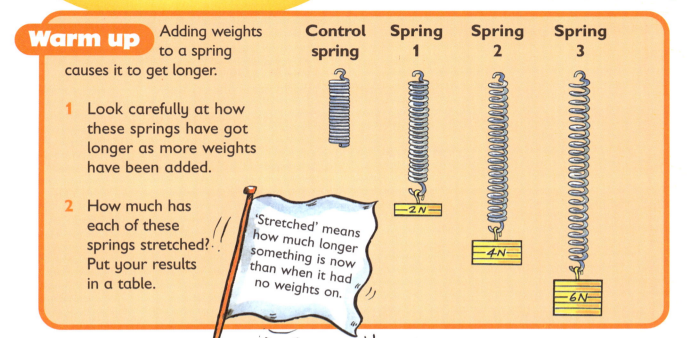

1. Look carefully at how these springs have got longer as more weights have been added.

2. How much has each of these springs stretched? Put your results in a table.

'Stretched' means how much longer something is now than when it had no weights on.

Lift off

A good way of showing results is to draw a graph. This will make any patterns much clearer. Graphs need to be drawn carefully.

1. Draw a graph showing what happens to the length of the spring as weights are added.

2. Are there any anomalous results? If so, what do you think this result should have been?

The booster

You can use the graph to predict the length of the spring for other weights. You need to be a little more skilful to do this.

1. What length would the spring be with these weights on it?

   a 10 N   b 14 N   c 20 N

2. Add these predicted readings to your graph.

Checkpoint

Now let's see if you can use the graph to write a scientific relationship.

Write a scientific relationship which tells you how adding weights stretches the spring. Use comparing words like 'bigger', 'smaller', 'shorter' and 'longer' to help you.

35

Shadows ☆

Scientific writing is accurate and uses the right scientific words

Warm up

Shadows are formed when light is blocked by a material.

1 Make a shadow using a torch. Talk about what you did and what you saw happening. Use these words when talking about your shadows.

light source   blocked   bright   dark   beam   travelling   sharp

2 Make a list of other words that you used to help describe what you observed.

Lift off

You can also change the size of shadows.

1 Use your torch to make a shadow of different sizes. To do this, you will need to change the distance between the torch and the object. Then put your results in a table like this:

How far the object is from the light source (cm)						
The size of the shadow (cm)						

2 Describe the pattern you have found in your results. Use words such as 'nearer', 'farther', 'bigger' and 'smaller' in your description.

The booster

You can always improve your writing by looking at what you have just done and redrafting. Start by making a first draft.

Write a first draft of how you made the shadow and changed its size. Use some of these sentences to help structure your writing.

> Before you make a shadow, you need to ...
> Then you need to ...
> After that, you ...
> If you want to make the shadow bigger, you ...
> You can put your results in a table, which is set out to show ...
> The results in our table made sense and told us that ...
> We have found out that ... you need to ...

Checkpoint

Now let's see if you can improve on your first draft.

Rewrite your account, trying to make it more concise and accurate and using scientific words.

Paths of light ⭐⭐

Ray diagrams show how light travels

Warm up
Which of the following are sources of light?

- the Sun
- a flower
- aluminium foil
- the Moon
- fire
- a candle
- a mirror
- a television

Lift off
For the boy to see the cat, light rays from a source must bounce off the cat and go into his eyes.

Which of these diagrams shows how the boy sees the cat?

The booster
There is one big mistake in each of these ray diagrams.

Light rays are drawn as straight lines. There is one arrowhead in the middle, which shows the direction the light travels.

Explain why each diagram is wrong.

Checkpoint
Now let's see if you can draw ray diagrams of your own.

Draw diagrams to show how:

a light travels from the Sun to a tree and into your eyes
b you can see around a corner using a mirror
c you see yourself in a mirror
d you see the Moon
e a shadow is formed.

37

Shadows/reflections ⭐⭐

Shadows and reflections are formed in different ways

Warm up
Work with your friends to try this.
1. Make some shadows using a torch.
2. Then look at some reflections in shiny surfaces, such as mirrors and spoons.
3. What is the main difference between a shadow and a reflection?

Lift off
Shadows are not the same as reflections. Here are some statements about shadows and reflections.

1. Decide whether each statement refers to a shadow or a reflection.
   - a Formed when light is blocked by an object
   - b Always dark in shape
   - c Formed when light is reflected
   - d The image swaps the details, left to right
   - e Seen on opaque surfaces
   - f Formed on shiny surfaces
   - g You can see no detail at all
   - h Shows a lifelike image

2. Make a table to organise the information correctly.

The booster
Look very carefully at these shadows and reflections. Something is not quite right!

1. Can you spot the any mistakes in how each of them has been formed?

2. Redraw the shadow and reflection in the way they would really appear.

Checkpoint
See if you can explain how shadows and reflections are formed.

Write a few sentences in your own words to explain how shadows are different from reflections.

Predicting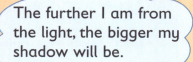

Graphs can be used to check your predictions

Warm up

Last night, Euan noticed that the size of his shadow changed as he walked down the street. He started to wonder if there might be a pattern between the size of his shadow and the distance he was from the streetlight. Here are some of his ideas.

The further I am from the light, the bigger my shadow will be.

The further I am from the light, the smaller my shadow will be.

The size of my shadow has nothing to do with how far I am from the light.

What would your prediction be? Write an 'I think … because …' sentence.

Lift off

Here are some results of Euan's investigation to show how the size of his shadow changed as he moved further away from the light.

Distance between the streetlight and Euan (m)	10	20	30	40	50
Length of his shadow (m)	2.0	2.4	3.8	5.0	4.5

Plot the results in a line graph. Make sure you label the *x*- and *y*-axes correctly. Be neat and careful.

The booster

Graphs can be used to help you see if a prediction as correct.

1. What pattern does your graph show?
2. Does it support any of Euan's predictions?

Checkpoint

If your prediction was right, you should be able to answer this question:

How big would Euan's shadow be if he were 45 metres away from the streetlight?

Improving explanations ⭐⭐

Some explanations are better than others

Warm up

Writing a good explanation takes practice.

1 Finish these two sentences:
   a I can see myself in a mirror because …
   b I can see light from a torch because …

2 Compare your answers with those of your friends. Who has written the best explanations?

Lift off

Good explanations give a sensible reason for *why* something happens.

1 Match the observation in the first column with the best reason in the second column. The first one is done for you.

   You cannot see around corners because — light is blocked.
   You can see yourself in a mirror because — light enters your eyes.
   Opaque objects make shadows because — light travels in straight lines.
   You can see light sources because — light is reflected.

2 Then write out the complete explanation linking the two parts together.

The booster

Correct science has to be used when writing explanations. Can you spot what is wrong in these explanations?

a Reflections are made because light is blocked by a material.
b You can see the Moon because the light it produces enters your eyes.
c Some objects look dull because they reflect light from their surfaces well.
d Shadows are shortest around midday because the Sun shines brightest then.

Rewrite each explanation giving the accurate scientific reason.

Checkpoint

Now let's see if you can understand why some explanations are better then others.

1 Read these two explanations carefully.
   ● Cardboard makes a dark shadow and plastic a light shadow because cardboard is an opaque material whilst plastic is a translucent material.
   ● A dark shadow is made when light is blocked by cardboard because this is an opaque material and no light passes through it. The shadow made by plastic is less dark because this material lets a little light through.

2 Give two reasons why the second explanation is better than the first one.

Electrical words

You need to know the meanings of some technical words to talk about electricity well

Warm up

Make a glossary of words which are all to do with electrical circuits. Here are two to get you started.

> Cell
> A device that changes chemical energy into electrical energy. Cells are used in electrical circuits. They come in different sizes and have a positive (+) and a negative (−) terminal at each end.
>
> Conductor
> A material is an electrical conductor if it lets electricity flow through it.

These words will help, but add as many of your own as you can.

insulator   circuit   current   voltage

Lift off

These ideas all refer to a simple electrical circuit.

1. Link the phrases in the two columns to make sensible sentences.

A simple circuit can be made from	make the bulb brighter.
In order for the circuit to work,	they all have to be connected together.
The bulb will be brighter	the bulb will burn out.
The brightness of the bulb	a cell, some wires, a switch and a bulb.
If there is a break in the circuit,	the circuit will not work.
Two cells will	if you use more cells.
However, if you use too many cells,	depends on the number of cells you use.

2. Rewrite the complete sentences in the correct order to make a paragraph.

The booster

Use your knowledge of how circuits work to add another paragraph to illustrate other ways in which the brightness of bulbs might be changed in a circuit.

Checkpoint

See how well you can use words to talk about electrical circuits.

Draw a cartoon strip that would enable your friend to construct circuits to show that the brightness of a bulb can be increased by adding more cells into a circuit.

41

Electrical symbols

Each electrical component has its own symbol

Warm up

Symbols are used every day to represent objects and places or to give warnings.

What do these everyday symbols mean? Add two more of your own.

a

b

c

Lift off

Each electrical component has its own symbol, and each one must be drawn correctly.

Write down what these electrical symbols mean.

a   b   c   d   e

The booster

Sometimes people make mistakes when drawing electrical symbols.

1 What is wrong with each of these electrical symbols?

a   b 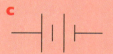   c   d

2 Draw each one correctly.

Checkpoint

Let's see if you know the correct symbols for electrical components.

1 Draw the correct electrical symbol for:

   a a 1.5 v cell   b a connecting wire   c a lamp (bulb)

   d a switch   e a 4.5 v battery

2 Draw one way in which each of these is often drawn incorrectly.

Drawing circuits ⭐⭐

Circuit diagrams are drawn as rectangles using the correct symbols

Warm up

It is easier to draw circuits using symbols rather than trying to draw the components as they really are.

1. Draw a circuit that contains a cell, a bulb, a switch and its connecting wires as it looks in real life.
2. Now draw the same circuit using the correct electrical symbols.

Lift off

The symbols used to draw each component in a circuit must be correct. The circuit also needs to be complete before it will work.

Both of these circuits will not work. Draw them again so that they will work.

a 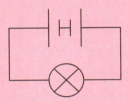   b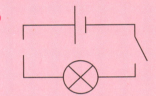

The booster

Scientists usually draw circuit diagrams in a rectangle. This helps to set out the circuit clearly so it is easier to understand.

Redraw these two circuit diagrams in a rectangle, just as a scientist would.

a    b

Checkpoint

Let's see if you can draw electrical circuits correctly using these three diagrams.

Each of these circuits has at least one mistake in it. Draw each one correctly.

a 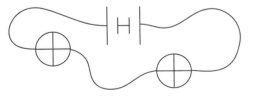   b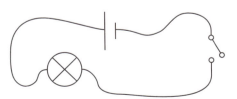

43

Matching circuits ⭐⭐

The number of bulbs and cells in a circuit affects the brightness of the bulbs

Warm up

For circuits to work, they must be complete with no gaps. They must also have a power supply and a device, such as a bulb, that uses the electrical energy.

Predict the brightness of the bulbs in these two circuits. Give good reasons for your answers.

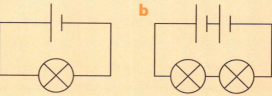

Lift off

Circuits can contain different numbers of cells, bulbs and batteries. If you keep the number of cells the same but change the number of bulbs, the brightness of the bulbs changes.

1. What will happen if the switch is closed in each of these circuits? Explain why.

2. What happens when the number of bulbs is the same as the number of cells used?

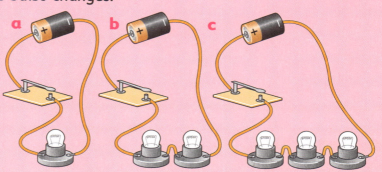

The booster

If you keep the number of bulbs the same but change the number of cells, this also changes the brightness of the bulbs.

1. What happens to the brightness of the bulbs as more cells are added?

2. What happens when the number of bulbs is the same as the number of cells used?

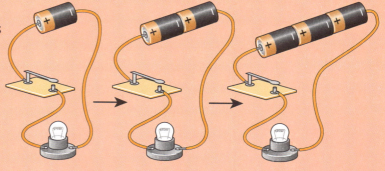

Checkpoint

Let's see if you can write a rule to sum this up.

How is the number of cells related to the brightness of the bulb in a circuit?

44

Controlling with switches

Switches can be used to control circuits

Warm up

Switches in a household circuit are used to control lights and other devices.

1. Does your home have any switches that:
   a. turn a light on and off from one place only?
   b. turn a light on and off from different places?
   c. work by pulling a string?

2. Discuss with your teacher or friend where you would find the different kinds of switches in your home.

Lift off

Switches can be used to operate a circuit in different ways.

1. Build these two circuits, putting the switches in the correct places.

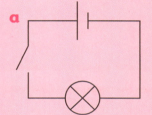 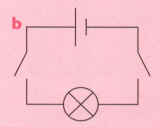

2. What is the main difference between the two circuits?
3. Write a sentence to describe what you need to do to make each one work.

The booster

These household circuits are more complicated.

1. Use your knowledge of switches and circuits to build them.

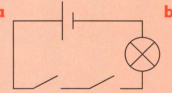 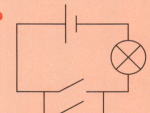

2. Explain what you have to do to the switches to make each circuit work.

Checkpoint

Let's see if you understand how switches can be used.

Which of the circuits in 'The booster' would be suitable for:
a. an alarm that can be switched on from different places?
b. a machine which is only turned on if another switch in a safety device is also on?

Confusing words ☆

Words can be confusing for different reasons

Warm up

Some science words are often spelled wrongly. Here are a few, but be careful — one word is only misspelled in a science context!

> **metel   gavrity   pray   skelaton   overy**
> **prediktion   circit   resistence   temperiture   preditor**

Write out the correct spelling for each word.

Lift off

Some words mean one thing in science and another in everyday life.

> **cell   solution   pure   suited   key**

1 Write a sentence to explain what each of the words in the box means in everyday life.

2 Write a second sentence to explain their scientific meaning.

The booster

Some words are easy to confuse even though they are very different.

Match the word in the first column with its correct meaning in the second.

Word	Meaning
melt	An image of something on a shiny surface.
dissolve	A material that takes the shape of the container by spreading.
shadow	A living thing that eats other animals or plants.
reflection	A material that holds its own shape and volume and doesn't flow.
producer	When a solid changes into a liquid because of a temperature rise.
consumer	A material that doesn't hold its own shape or volume.
solid	An outline of an object, formed when light is blocked by the object.
liquid	A living thing that makes food for itself and others feed off it.
gas	When a solid or liquid forms a mixture with another liquid.

Checkpoint

Now let's see if you can sort out some more words. Explain the difference between:

a a predator and its prey   b transparent, translucent and opaque.

Glossary

Adaptation
The way in which plants and animals are suited to their particular habitat.

Air resistance
The name given to the friction force that is caused when an object moves through the air. It tries to stop or slow down the object from moving.

Carnivore
An animal that eats other animals.

Cell
A device that changes chemical into electrical energy. It has a positive (+) and a negative (–) terminal for connection to the circuit.

Circuit
A closed loop that allows current to flow round. The circuit starts and ends with the cell or battery.

Consumer
Animals are all consumers because they eat plants or other animals.

Energy
You use this when you do work like climbing the stairs, lifting a bag or playing a game. You also need it for growing.

Force
A push, pull, twist or turn. Gravity, friction, air and water resistance are all examples of forces. The units of force are Newtons (N).

Friction
The name given to the force that occurs when two objects move over each other.

Gas
One of the three states of matter. Any air-like substance that moves freely to fill the space available.

Gravity
The name of a force of attraction that acts on all objects on Earth. It pulls the objects towards the centre of the Earth. Gravity also acts on other planets and very large objects.

Herbivore
Animals that eat plants.

Irreversible change
A change made to a material that cannot be reversed. Burning paper is an example of irreversible change. When paper burns, it makes ash, carbon dioxide and water. You cannot get the paper back once it has burned.

Liquid
One of the three states of matter. Liquids like water can flow and take up the shape of any container they are put in.

Mass
The name given to the amount of material in an object. An object's mass is always the same. It is measured in grams.

Micro-organism
Very small living organisms, such as bacteria, that can only be seen with a microscope.

Newton
The unit of force. It is named after the English scientist Sir Isaac Newton who first put together ideas about forces.

Producer
Plants are called producers because they use energy from the Sun to make their own food.

Reversible change
A change made to a material that can be easily reversed. Melting, freezing, evaporating and condensing are all examples of reversible changes. These things happen naturally all the time.

Solid
One of the three states of matter. Any material that is a solid is usually hard and has a shape that can only be changed if you hit it hard.

Switch
A break in an electrical circuit that can be controlled. The current flows when the switch is closed and stops when the switch is open.

Published by Letts Educational
The Chiswick Centre
414 Chiswick High Road
London W4 5TF
Telephone: 020 8996 3333
Fax: 020 8742 8390
E-mail: mail@lettsed.co.uk
Website: www.letts-education.com

Letts Educational is part of the Granada Learning Group.
Granada Learning is a division of Granada plc.

© Alan Jarvis and William Merrick 2003

First published 2003

ISBN 1 84085 9350

The authors assert the moral right to be identified as the authors
of this work.

All rights reserved. No part of this publication may be reproduced,
stored in a retrieval system, or transmitted, in any form or by any
means electronic, mechanical, photocopying, recording or
otherwise, without the prior permission of the Publisher or a
licence permitting restricted copying in the United Kingdom issued
by the Copyright Licensing Agency Ltd, 90 Tottenham Court Road,
London W1P 9HE. This book is sold subject to the condition that it
shall not by way of trade or otherwise be lent, hired out or
otherwise circulated without the publisher's prior consent.

British Library Cataloguing in Publication Data
A catalogue record for this book is available from the British Library.

This book was designed and produced for Letts Educational by
Ken Vail Graphic Design, Cambridge

Commissioned by Kate Newport

Project management by Phillipa Allum

Editing by Nancy Candlin

Illustrations by Graham-Cameron Illustration (Pat Murray)

Production by PDQ

Printed and bound in Italy by Amilcare Pizzi